Written by Gurj Bassi

Edited by Philippa Wingate
Designed by Zoe Quayle
Production by Joanne Rooke
Picture Research by Judith Palmer

Picture Acknowledgements
Front cover: PA Photos
Back cover: CLA/LFI

Sharjo/expresspictures.com: pages 38/39
Paul David Drabble/FAMOUS: pages 24, 27
Justin Goff/Disney: pages 42/43
CAB/LFI: pages 34, 57
CLA/LFI: pages 8/9, 11, 20/21, 54/55
LARK/LFI: pages 2/3, 13, 15, 17, 62/63
Redferns: pages 30/31
Chapman/REX FEATURES: page 33
James Curley/REX FEATURES: pages 50/51
Tony Larkin/REX FEATURES: page 6
Brian Rasic/REX FEATURES: pages 28, 47, 58

First published in Great Britain in 2004 by Buster Books,
an imprint of Michael O'Mara Books Limited,
9 Lion Yard, Tremadoc Road,
London SW4 7NQ

Copyright © 2004 Buster Books

All rights reserved.
No part of this book may be reproduced, stored in a retrieval system,
or transmitted in any form or by any means, electronic, mechanical,
photocopying, recording or otherwise without the prior
written permission of the copyright owners.

A CIP catalogue record for this book is available from the British Library.

ISBN: 1-904613-73-X

1 3 5 7 9 10 8 6 4 2

Printed and bound in Italy by L.E.G.O.

McFLY
Unauthorized
Annual 2005

CONTENTS

- 8 The Fab Four
- 10 Tom – Funny McFly
- 12 Harry – Flirty McFly
- 14 Danny – Party McFly
- 16 Dougie – Shy McFly
- 18 Off To A McFlying Start
- 22 Early Promise
- 25 Wordsearch
- 26 Nu-pop
- 29 Singing Their Praises
- 32 McFly On McFly
- 35 Crossword
- 36 The McFly Residence
- 40 Fact File
- 44 Girls, Girls, Girls
- 48 Who's For You?
- 52 Style Secrets
- 54 Cringe!
- 56 Original Pranksters
- 59 McFan Or McPhoney?
- 60 Back To The Future

THE FAB FOUR
MCFLY

Armed with cheeky grins, bundles of talent, and fiercely melodic tunes, bouncy guitar boys McFly crash-landed smack-bang in the middle of the pop world in 2004. And boy did they make a dent in it! Tom Fletcher, Dougie Poynter, Harry Judd and Danny Jones had arrived to put the fizz back into pop.

In March 2004, a mass of wristbands, spiky bleached hair, and oversized cropped jeans eclipsed the charts for two whole weeks. McFly's fantastic debut single, '5 Colours In Her Hair', rocketed straight into the number-one spot. No one could resist their infectious choruses, cheeky-chappie attitudes, and the fact that they are really cute helped a little too! Their energy was contagious and before long, McFly mania swept the nation.

The boys hit the road on a sell-out tour with their mates from Busted.

They dominated magazine covers and accumulated a fan base in record time. The McFly fellas strapped themselves on board a rollercoaster ride to stardom... and haven't looked back since.

So get your air guitars at the ready as we take a look at the success story of the year – the fab four that are McFly.

Are you ready for take-off?

TOM McFLY
FUNNY McFLY

NAME: Tom Fletcher (guitar and vocals)
DATE OF BIRTH: 17 July 1985
PLACE OF BIRTH: Harrow
STAR SIGN: Cancer
EYES: Brown
SIBLINGS: One little sister named Kerry
FURRY FRIENDS: A dog called Christmas
FAVOURITE ACTORS: Tom Hanks, Katie Holmes
FAVOURITE FILMS: *The Beach, Vanilla Sky, Almost Famous, The Shawshank Redemption, Back to the Future, Ghostbusters*
FAVOURITE TV PROGRAMMES: *Friends, Dawson's Creek*
FAVOURITE SONG: Fun Fun Fun/Superman (Five for Fighting)
FAVOURITE BAND: The Beach Boys
FAVOURITE MALE SINGERS: Tom Delonge (Blink 182) and Justin Timberlake
FAVOURITE FEMALE SINGER: Avril Lavigne

FIRST GIG: Bryan Adams
FAVOURITE DRINK: Grape and melon high-juice
FAVOURITE FOOD: Pizza, pop tarts
DREAM CAR: Mini Cooper – all he has at the moment is a Fiat Punto
IDOLIZES: The Beach Boys and his dad
DESCRIBES HIMSELF AS: Honest
ONE THING HE ALWAYS CARRIES WITH HIM: A plectrum
ANYTHING ELSE?: He wees in swimming pools! He hates Wednesdays. "They're always pretty lame. The TV's rubbish and it's only the middle of the week. Wednesdays suck!" His favourite subjects at school were art, music and science.

HARRY FLIRTY McFLY

NAME: Harry Judd (drums) nickname Juddy Harold
DATE OF BIRTH: 23 December 1985
PLACE OF BIRTH: Chelmsford
STAR SIGN: Capricorn
EYES: Blue
SIBLINGS: One older brother and one older sister
FURRY FRIENDS: A gerbil named Travis, a black Labrador named Percy, a Jack Russell named Tilly, five chickens, and a cat named Molly
FAVOURITE ACTORS: Jim Carrey, Jennifer Aniston
FAVOURITE FILM: *Ace Ventura – Pet Detective*
FAVOURITE TV PROGRAMMES: *Friends, The Office*
FAVOURITE SONG: 'Hey Jude' by The Beatles
FAVOURITE BANDS: The Used, Blink 182, The Beatles
FAVOURITE MALE SINGER: Chris Cornell
FAVOURITE FEMALE SINGER: Alanis Morissette
FIRST GIG: A Doors tribute band
FAVOURITE DRINK: Apple juice
FAVOURITE FOOD: His Mum's spaghetti
DREAM CAR: Ford Capri
IDOLIZES: His parents and Travis Barker from Blink 182. Harry was so star-struck when he met Blink 182, he almost fainted!
DESCRIBES HIMSELF AS: Lazy, sarcastic and always trying to have a laugh
ONE THING HE ALWAYS CARRIES WITH HIM: A pair of drumsticks
ANYTHING ELSE?: Enjoys clicking his fingers and picking his spots. "I love bursting them!" Loves spending time with his friends. His favourite sport is cricket, and his favourite subject at school was art.

DANNY PARTY McFLY

NAME:	Danny Jones (guitar and vocals)
DATE OF BIRTH:	12 March 1986
PLACE OF BIRTH:	Bolton
STAR SIGN:	Pisces
EYES:	Blue
SIBLINGS:	One older sister named Vicky
FURRY FRIENDS:	A gerbil named Bruce and two police dogs
FAVOURITE ACTOR:	Adam Sandler
FAVOURITE FILM:	*E.T.*
FAVOURITE TV PROGRAMME:	*Police, Camera, Action!*
FAVOURITE SONG:	'Born In The USA' by Bruce Springsteen
FAVOURITE BANDS:	Bruce Springsteen and The E-Street Band or The Who
FAVOURITE MALE SINGERS:	Bruce Springsteen, Kelly Joe Phelps, John Mayer
FAVOURITE FEMALE SINGERS:	Eva Cassidy or Alanis Morissette
FIRST GIG:	Bruce Springsteen
FAVOURITE DRINK:	Grape and melon high-juice
FAVOURITE FOOD:	Spaghetti bolognese, warm cookies, cake and chocolate eclairs
DREAM CAR:	Lamborghini
IDOLIZES:	His uncle Andy, his parents and Bruce Springsteen
DESCRIBES HIMSELF AS:	Innocent, never stressed and chatty
ONE THING HE ALWAYS CARRIES WITH HIM:	A plectrum
ANYTHING ELSE?:	He bites his nails. He once found a purse full of cash on the bus and handed it in to the police, but after two weeks they gave it back to him because no one claimed it. He was quids in! His favourite words are 'homodom' and 'rat leg'.

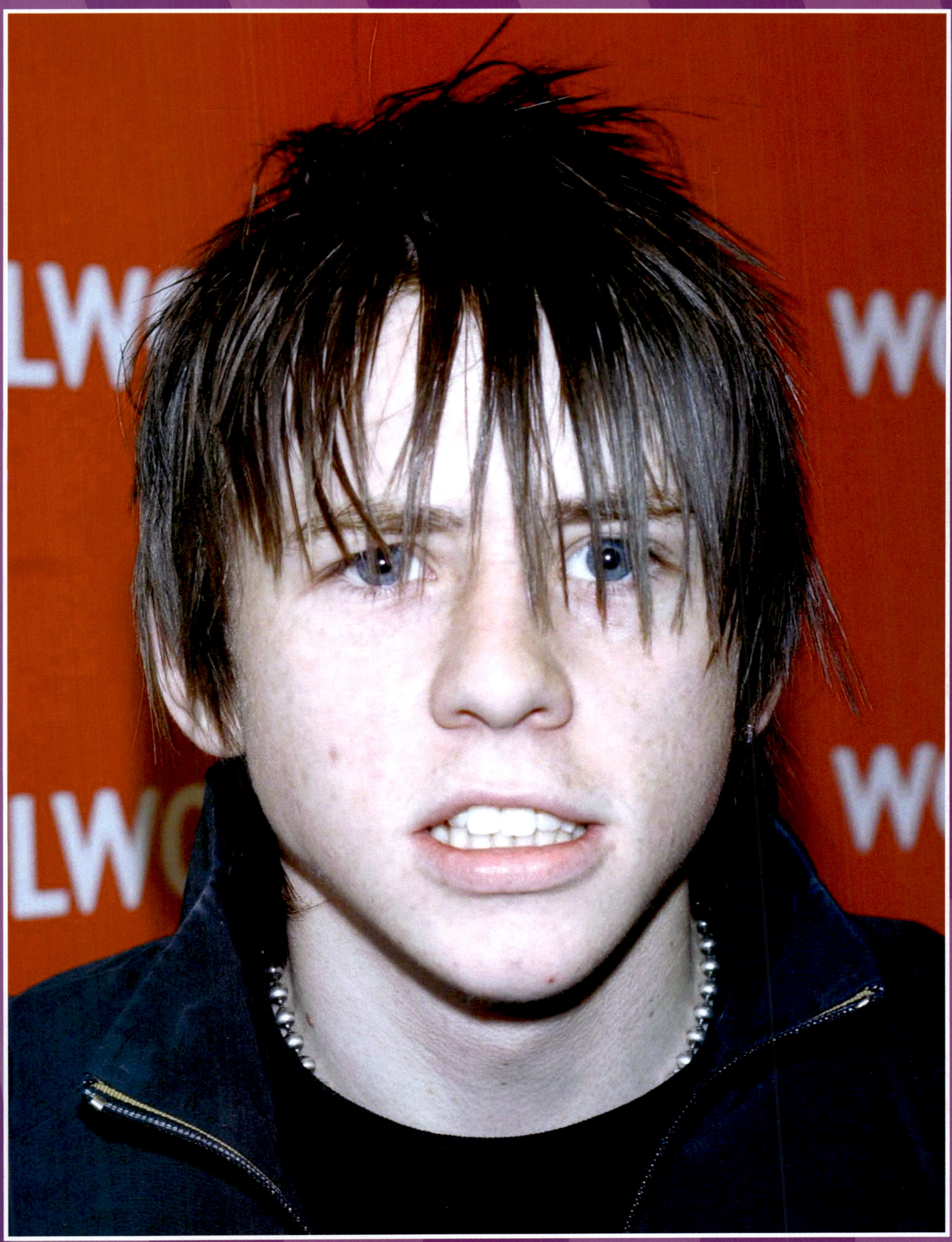

DOUGIE SHY McFLY

NAME: Dougie Poynter (bass)
DATE OF BIRTH: 30 November 1987
PLACE OF BIRTH: Orsett
STAR SIGN: Sagittarius
EYES: Greeny blue
SIBLINGS: One sister called Jazzy
FURRY FRIENDS: Dougie has his own mini-zoo – two lizards called Zuki and Buffy, two cats called Moff and CJ, two dogs called Meggy and Fraser and a frog, Ned
FAVOURITE ACTORS: Brad Pitt, Hilary Duff or "anyone fit"!
FAVOURITE FILM: *Urethra Chronicals* by Blink 182
FAVOURITE TV PROGRAMME: Anything on *MTV*
FAVOURITE SONG: 'Don't Tell Me It's Over' by Blink 182
FAVOURITE BAND: Blink 182
FAVOURITE MALE SINGER: Tom Delonge (Blink 182)
FAVOURITE FEMALE SINGER: Amy Lee (Evanescence)
FIRST GIG: Wet Wet Wet
FAVOURITE DRINK: Lucozade
FAVOURITE FOOD: Greek and all types of seafood
IDOLIZES: Blink 182
DESCRIBES HIMSELF AS: A dark horse
ONE THING HE ALWAYS CARRIES WITH HIM: A plectrum
ANYTHING ELSE?: Bad habits include not cutting his toenails, not washing his hair, and eating dead skin! But it's not just his own dead skin he likes to feed on, he munches other people's dead skin too! "When I went on holiday with Tom, and James from Busted, I ate dead skin from James's back," he enthuses. The closest thing he has to a favourite sport is spying on Harry at night! His favourite word is 'rad' (meaning cool).

OFF TO A McFLYING START

The birth of this pop phenomenon began way back in 2000, and here's how it all happened:

• Tom narrowly missed out to Charlie Simpson for a place in the final line-up of Busted. "I was really disappointed," he recalls.

• In 2002, Tom met Bolton boy Danny, who used to play cover versions of Richard Ashcroft songs in pubs and clubs. They both turned up at the same audition for a new boy band, except neither one of them realized it was to be an all-singing, all-dancing boy band. They got chatting and discovered they both shared a love for 60s music, and kept in contact.

• Busted's managers decided to sign up Tom as a songwriter and he became good pals with the Busted boys. He even co-wrote half of their second album, *A Present For Everyone*.

• An advert was placed in weekly music bible *NME* to find three supremely talented lads to join Tom and form an ensemble similar to Busted, but different enough to earn their own success.

• For Danny, fate had finally come calling. He successfully made it into the band. Tom and Danny clicked instantly and began collaborating on a series of songs that would sow the seeds of the McFly sound.

• A few months later, the line-up was completed with Harry and Dougie. "Loads of people turned up at the auditions and loads of them were really bad!" remembers Danny. "We narrowed it down to two drummers and two bass players, but Dougie and Harry stood out."

• The quartet moved into a house in North London, with James from Busted, and spent a year honing their skills before they were presented to Universal, the record company.

• Paul Adams at Universal was so impressed by what he saw and heard that he signed the boys up straight away.

"I was completely blown away," he remembers. "Every once in a while, you come across a band that you know will be huge, and McFly is that band."

- In late 2003, a huge buzz began to form around McFly as they were presented to the country's media. Needless to say, the media loved them, and McFly were tipped for big things in 2004.

- McFly had their first taste of the number-one spot before they had even released their own single. In November 2003, they joined label-mates Busted on the flipside of 'Crashed The Wedding', for a fiery romp through 'Build Me Up Buttercup'.

- In February 2004, McFly joined Busted on a sell-out arena tour. "It was a bit of a shock to be honest, when the curtain went up on the first night," says Danny. "Just all these people stretching out before you. But it was absolutely brilliant, we loved it."

- On 29 March 2004, McFly released their debut single, '5 Colours In Her Hair'. It blasted straight to number one and stayed there for two weeks. McFly were the first act of 2004 to last longer than one week at the top of the charts.

And the rest, as they say, is history!

WHAT'S IN A NAME?

Why 'McFly'? Tom named the band after Michael J. Fox's character in the 1980s cult movie, *Back To The Future*. Danny also had something to do with it – "Basically I was with Busted when they soundchecked for 'Year 3000'," explains Tom. "And the name sort of sprang into my head. Danny didn't like it at first, but then we watched the film, and there's a bit where Biff crashes into the side of a manure truck, and it had Danny's name on the side of the manure truck. That was it, that was the turning point!"

EARLY PROMISE

McFly are super-talented boys. While most bands have a team of people to write songs and play instruments for them, McFly do it all themselves. In fact, music has always played a huge part in the boys' lives. Here's the low-down on their musical influences, when they first picked up an instrument and how they got hooked...

Danny

Danny's been playing the guitar since he was six years old. "It's great to learn instruments when you're a bit younger," he says. "But it's never too late!"

He grew up listening to American rock, but he says the real reason he picked up a guitar was his uncle. "He's an amazing guitarist and I wanted to be able to play just like him. I had a private tutor... I started to learn the violin too, but I wasn't any good."

Danny's talents don't just stop at the guitar, he can also play the drums, ukulele, harmonica and accordion!

Harry

When he was growing up, Harry didn't really idolize drummers and never wanted to be a drummer himself. He just kind of fell into it. "A few of my mates were in a band. I went to watch them and I started messing about on the drums," he remembers. "My friend Sam was the only drummer in my year at school, because everyone else played guitar or bass. So I emailed him and asked him to teach me a simple beat."

During the following Easter break from boarding school, Harry bought his first drum kit. "I taught myself by drumming along to CDs. My brother played drums too, so he taught me a few things."

When Harry returned to school the same term, he persuaded his parents to let him have drumming lessons. From then on he honed his skills to such an impressive level that they landed him a place in McFly!

Tom

Believe it or not, Tom didn't even start listening to pop music until he was sixteen. He preferred bands from the 1960s, such as The Beatles or The Beach Boys. And considering he does the majority of the songwriting in McFly, it'll come as even more of a surprise that Tom didn't start writing songs until he was seventeen.
"I only started writing songs when I met James [from Busted]. In fact, James taught me everything I know about songwriting."

But let's rewind to when Tom was still a toddler. He taught himself how to play the guitar and drums. "I fell in love with the guitar as soon as I picked it up," he recalls. "I had my first lesson when I was five years old. I think everyone should learn an instrument. It's great!"

Dougie

Dougie spent his early teen years listening to lots of Californian punk bands, such as Blink 182 and New Found Glory, and he's still a fan to this day. In fact, Dougie thanks Blink 182 for his toilet obsessed sense of humour! He idolizes their guitarist, Tom Delonge, and hopes to be just like him one day. "He's just such a dude!" enthuses Dougie.

Much like his band mates, Dougie was an early learner when it came to picking up an instrument. He's been playing the bass for as long as he can remember, which means it must've been an extremely early age, considering he's the youngest member of the band!

Dougie was a tender fifteen years old when he joined McFly, but his age was never an issue when it came to making it into the band. According to the others, at the McFly auditions no one else came close to matching Dougie's bass-playing ability. As Dougie himself would say, he was the dude!

WORDSEARCH MCFLY

D	E	C	V	N	L	B	D	A	N	N	Y	P	O	
M	O	T	E	N	J	U	B	M	S	A	C	N	Q	
F	I	H	C	Y	B	U	S	T	E	D	S	R	L	
U	A	E	L	P	H	N	J	H	R	T	A	S	V	
P	C	F	X	A	S	E	C	V	O	T	F	I	H	
D	C	A	M	O	R	P	E	Z	I	Q	L	M	G	
M	P	B	K	L	U	C	D	U	M	N	Y	W	D	
A	S	F	T	D	O	U	G	I	E	E	R	T	Y	
Z	J	O	U	H	L	B	M	T	M	D	U	N	Y	
C	P	U	T	W	O	Y	Z	F	D	S	N	M	I	
F	B	R	Q	W	C	X	K	L	Y	R	R	A	H	
B	S	K	A	T	E	R	B	O	Y	S	X	N	K	
G	V	Q	I	P	V	O	S	D	G	A	S	B	J	
S	R	O	B	V	I	O	U	S	L	Y	V	C	A	
Y	E	R	H	J	F	A	C	D	N	B	N	S	M	

Can you find the following McFly words in the grid above?

TOM
HARRY
DOUGIE
DANNY
MCFLY
GUITAR

FIVE COLOURS
SKATER BOYS
OBVIOUSLY
BUSTED
THE FAB FOUR

25

NU-POP McFLY

McFly take their music very seriously. Here are some of their thoughts on the style of their songs.

What is nu-pop?

The boys describe their music as "nu-pop". It's pop music, but unique pop. It's not the cheesy kind of stuff you'd find boy bands miming along to! "There are two sides to it," explains Dougie. "You've got the commercial pop side, and the gritty rock side."

According to Harry, nu-pop is a fusion between old and new, for granpops and minipops alike. "I'd say our sound has a 60s twist, with Busted-style lyrics." And like their mates Busted, McFly write all their own songs. That's something of a rarity among pop bands, but then again, as Tom states, "We are not just another manufactured act. We're a proper band, the same way The Beatles were a proper band. Our music speaks for itself."

Harry reckons it's very important that they get to perform and record songs they've written themselves. "It means we actually care what we're singing about," he says. "We wouldn't want to play our instruments in a band that played music written by someone else," Danny adds. "We're just trying to be ourselves. We're not trying to be anything else. And it's a really fun thing to do, actually – not just to be in a band, but to be in pop as well." And why is that? "Well, because you get all the screaming fans of course!" Danny remarks cheekily.

Number one!

The song responsible for propelling McFly to the top of the charts the moment they appeared on the pop scene was '5 Colours In Her Hair'. The track was penned by Tom and Danny, with some help from Busted's James.

It is, without a doubt, McFly's signature track. But who is the girl with five colours in her hair? Does she actually exist? The answer – yes, she does! The song was inspired by a Channel 4 soap called *As If*. "It's about this actress," explains Tom. "Her name's Emily Corrie, and she plays Sooz. Me and Danny really fancied her. On screen, she's got this no bull attitude, which is really attractive, but we met her in real life – without her dreadlocks and piercings – and it was a bit of a let-down really!" Fortunately, the single wasn't a disappointment at all.

When the song was released, it was so big that it even started a new trend. Danny reveals, "My mum's a hairdresser and she keeps getting all these girls coming in and asking for five colours in their hair! But she's so pleased, she does it for free!"

Making the video

To match the summertime, surfer vibes of '5 Colours In Her Hair', the video had a 1970s retro theme. The lads nicked some Beatles-cool, using the famous Abbey Road zebra crossing, and they had lots of girls in groovy outfits, dancing around them as they performed on a *Top Of The Pops*-like set. Of course, the video also starred an actual girl with five colours in her hair.

All four boys agree that shooting the video was one of the highlights of their pop careers. It will sit pretty in their memories for a long time to come.

Danny: "That video shoot has got to be one of the best days of my life. It was such a wicked day. We were full of adrenalin. But I don't think we realized how tiring it was until the next day, when we got up two hours late for the next filming session!"

Tom: "We got told off for that!"

Harry: "It was hard work though! There was a lot of waiting around and it was freezing."

Dougie: "We actually had a girl with five colours in her hair and loads of fit extras, too. I sat there thinking, 'I can't believe they're here for me!' – But they were, even if they didn't know who we were yet!"

SINGING THEIR PRAISES

McFly were destined for superstardom from day one, and even the music critics agreed.

The *Daily Star:* "McFly are prime examples of the new appetite for kicking power pop that looks like sealing the fate of pappy pretty-boy music."

Teen Now: "Pop's had an injection of street cred, and if the hype surrounding McFly is anything to go by, these boys are destined for big things. Forget reality TV stars – McFly are the future."

Bliss: "McFly are ready to stand on their own two feet, take the world of pop by the scruff of its neck, and shake it until it screams. Bring it on boys, we've been waiting for you!"

J17: "The hottest lads to hit the charts in 2004. The band have a foot firmly planted on the pop ladder."

Mizz: "Pay attention because these lads are about to rock your world!"

The *Evening Standard:* "McFly are proving that boy bands don't have to be bland."

The *Scotsman:* "McFly are putting the fizz back into pop."

Music Week: "McFly are a cracking pop unit – great all-round musicians, writers, performers and entertainers."

The *Sunday Mail:* "The most exciting prospects of 2004."

The *Guardian:* "Superstardom seems assured."

Girl: "Pop is about to turn a new corner!"

More: "They're cute as a button with a poptastic rockabilly twist. They're gonna be huge!"

Dare: "These lads have had loads of hype – but they live up to it with their cracking debut. Nice one McFly!"

Smash Hits: "'5 Colours In Her Hair' is perfect summery pop/rock!"

The *Daily Mirror:* "Brash, confident and outgoing, it's another nail in the boy-band coffin."

McFLY ON McFLY

No one knows the McFly guys better than they know each other, and here's what they *really* think of each other...

Tom
Danny: "Tom doesn't chat to fit birds enough. He's too shy. And sometimes he's a bit bossy, but he can be the nicest bloke in the world, too."

Dougie: "Tom's talented, immature and stinky. He's got bad breath! But mostly he's just bossy, he's like the Daddy of the band! He's very sensible."

Harry: "Tom cries at girlie films! He really blubbed at *Love Actually*! Ha ha! But he is actually the strongest member of the band by far – he's not a complete wuss."

Dougie
Tom: "Dougie's really quirky. He comes across as really quiet, but then he'll just come out with really weird stuff! It's funny! And he's got the cute, youthful looks."

Harry: "Dougie's very funny, not shy but he's quiet. Like, in the car, we'll be talking and he sits staring out the window. All you have to do is tap him!"

Danny: "Dougie's cool, but he used to faint when he got nervous!"

Harry
Tom: "Me and Harry are the mothers of the band, and the other two are like weird kids. Harry's got those handsome, model looks."

Dougie: "Harry's an amazing drummer and also very leader-ish. But he can be really grumpy sometimes. He moans about everything! He's quite posh, but he's not as posh as he used to be – we've dragged him down a bit to our level!"

Danny
Tom: "Danny's gormless! He's a really happy person, so if you're ever feeling a bit sad then he's the one you go to, because he's never in a bad mood. He's a kick-arse guitarist and everyone loves Danny. He's definitely got the most screaming girls after him!"

Harry: "Danny's definitely the naughtiest member of the band. He's really cheeky, but he cheers us up whenever we're tired. He's always in a good mood and he says stupid stuff without meaning to."

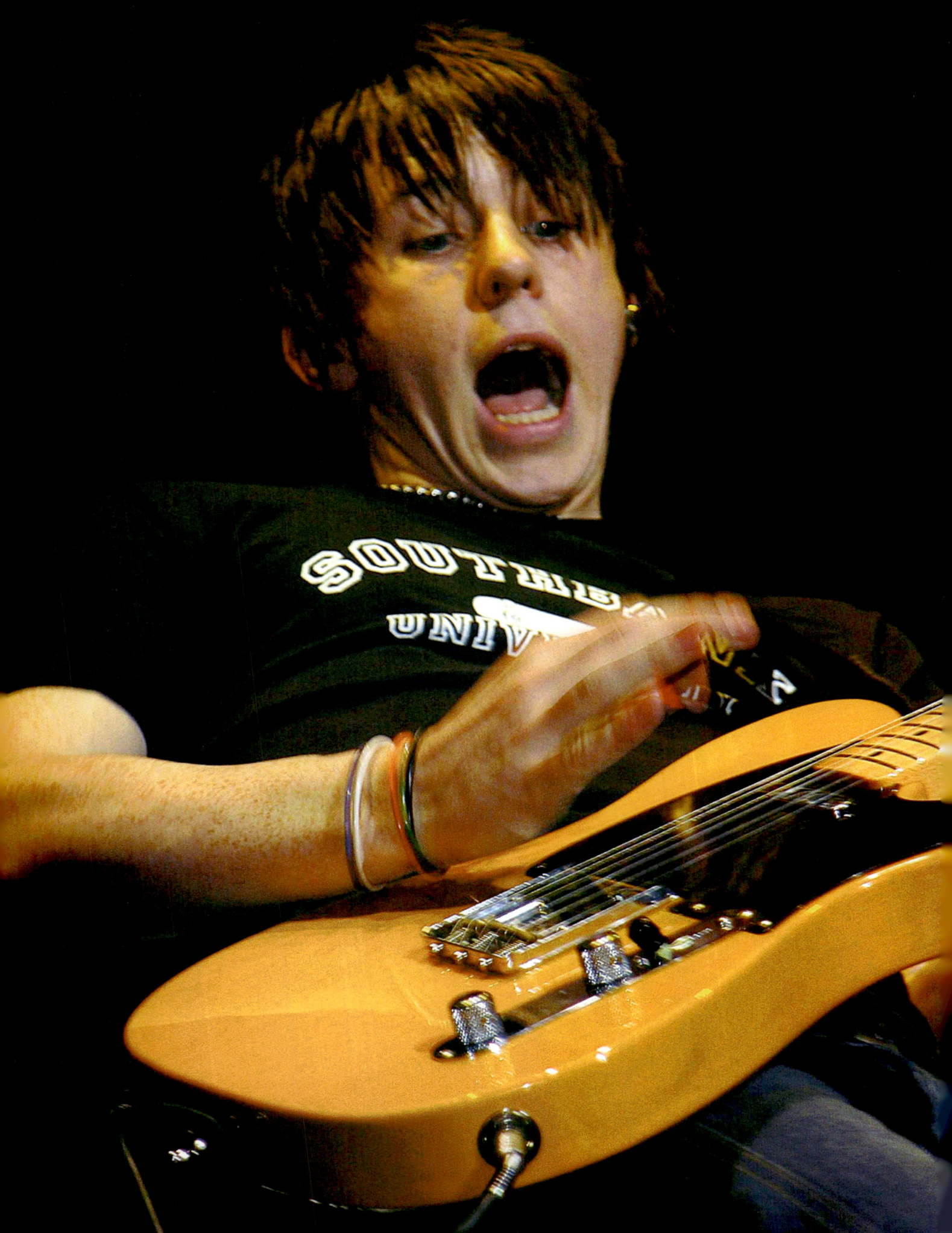

CROSSWORD

Here's a McFly crossword. You will find all the answers somewhere in this book, and you can check that you've got everything right on page 61.

ACROSS

1. The star sign of the youngest member of the band (11)
2. Dougie loves watching this channel (3)
3. All the members of the band love eating this food (5)
4. A facial feature that only Tom has (6)
7. The name of Tom's sister (5)
9. One of Danny's favourite words (7)
10. Harry has one named Molly (3)
13. An interesting instrument Danny knows how to play (7)
14. Harry has a pair in his bedroom (5,5)

DOWN

1. Dougie sometimes likes to sign his autograph in the shape of one (10)
5. What Dougie did before his audition for the band (5)
6. Harry got top marks for it at school (3)
8. The girl they sang about had five of these in her hair (7)
10. The poor person who has to tidy up the mucky McFly residence (7)
11. Danny has a crush on this Sugababe (5)
12. The month they released their debut single (5)

THE McFLY RESIDENCE

Q: What do you get if you cross one big house, no parents, and four rowdy boys?
A: Piles of smelly socks, lots of mouldy bread, and endless crazy antics!

On living together

Danny: "It's pretty cool, because we're just five teenagers hanging out together, with no parents around to tell us what to do!"

Harry: "The noisiest person in the house has to be Danny. We'll be watching TV, and he'll go to his room and play his music really loudly, strumming on his guitar and stamping his feet about. And when he talks, he shouts."

Dougie: "I've seen a lot of mouldy bread and even mouldy beans in our house. Once I opened a loaf of bread and the whole lot was green!"

Dougie: "I have the smallest room in our house. It was weird at first, because we didn't know each other and we were all living together, but we got used to it. We're like brothers now."

Tom: "I have the coolest room in our house. I have the whole third floor to myself, and I've got a little balcony, too."

Bedroom bits

Dougie has flower prints on his bedroom curtains, although he says they were already there when he moved in. Yeah, right!

Tom's room is actually the attic.

Danny has posters of Ocean Colour Scene and The Vines covering his bedroom walls. He also has his own McFly number plate hanging in his bedroom. "It was a present from my dad in Bolton," he explains. "When I first moved down I was homesick as I didn't go back home for about three months. He bought me it to cheer me up."

Harry has pictures of his old cricket team in his room, as well as a toy donkey that his sister gave him called Eeyore. He also has a few other stuffed animals named Pockets, Teddy and Monkey.

Dougie has posters of Frankie from S Club 8 covering his bedroom walls.

Tom sleeps on a real NASA space mattress; one that astronauts sleep on when they're in their rockets. He says, "It's really squishy. You just sink into it."

Harry has the messiest bedroom in the house, and says he shares it with "crumbs, bacteria and insects".

Forget posters of sexy ladies – Danny has posters of crinkly rocker Bruce Springsteen on his walls.

Harry has a pair of bongo drums in his bedroom.

House facts

• The lads aren't quite as talented when it comes to using pots and pans, as they are with their instruments. "We eat take-away pizzas loads, because it's easy," confesses Tom. Lazy boys!

• McFly's fridge is packed with lots of water and fruit, but it's not all healthy stuff. Harry says, "We've got beer, bacon, cheese and Marmite, too!"

• Each boy in the McFly house has his own bathroom and bathroom cabinet.

However, all that toiletry storage space is just wasted on them. "I only keep a toothbrush in my bathroom cabinet," says Dougie. Tom says he's not into lotions and potions, but Danny is, so his cabinets are packed with them. He has four bottles of aftershave!

• The McFly house is a mixture of flashy meets trashy from the sound of it. According to the lads, it's full of stolen traffic cones and road signs, but they also have a huge forty-inch TV screen with surround-sound.

• The boys are rubbish when it comes to cleaning that they have a cleaner who tidies up for them once a week.

• The guys live next door to an old people's home.

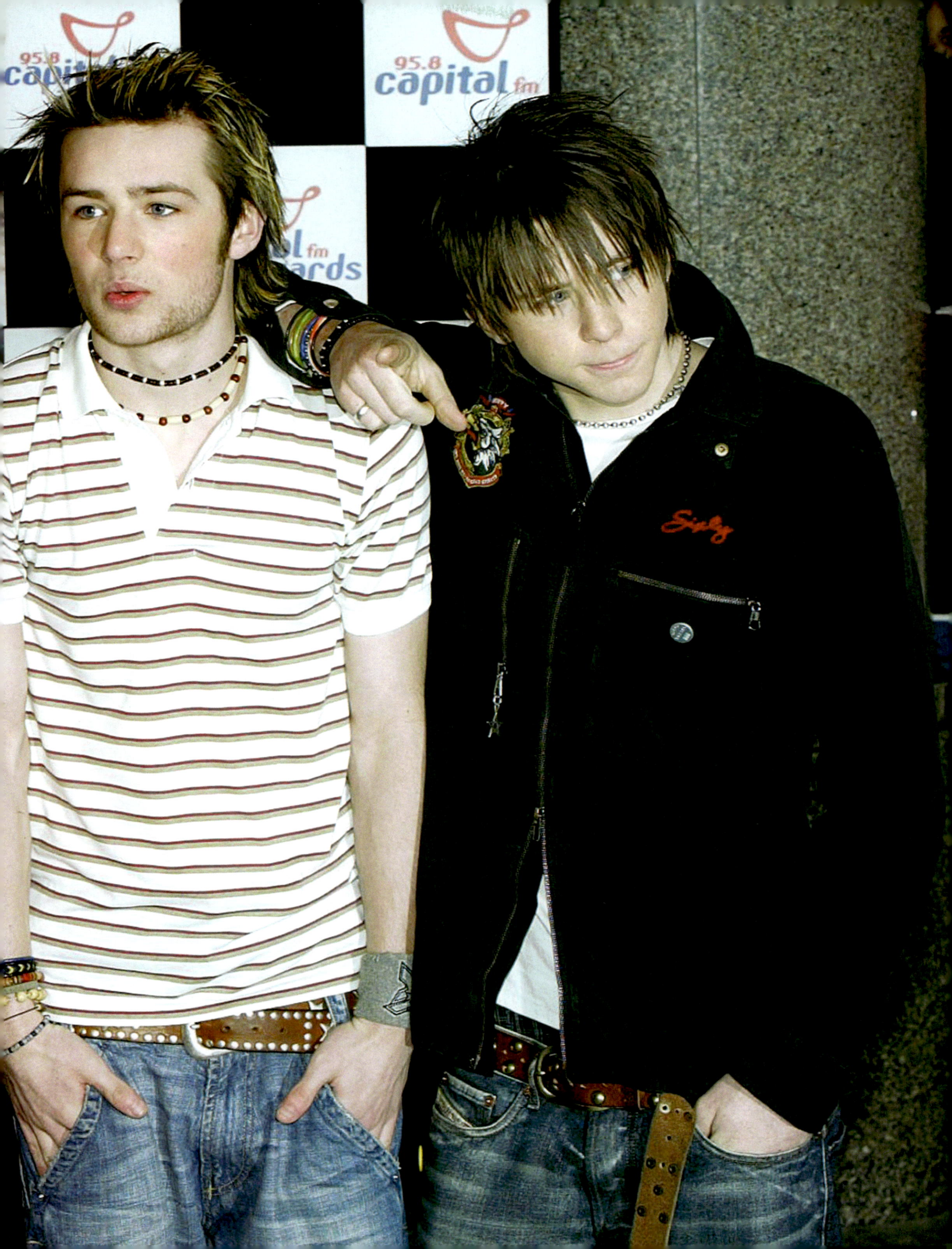
95.8
capital fm

FACT FILE McFLY

Here's a bumper fact file on the fabulous McFly four!

- Danny can blow bubbles with his tongue. How? "I curve my tongue, then blow through it," he reveals.
- Danny spent a whopping £4,000 on a studio with his first pay cheque.
- Tom has gone a whole week without changing his boxers. He justifies himself with the following theory, "You don't need clean ones unless you're seeing a girl."
- Tom was the first member of McFly to pass his driving test.
- Harry attended a very posh boarding school called Uppingham. He was a few years below Charlie from Busted.
- Dougie loves crowd surfing. The first time he did it was at a New Found Glory concert.
- Harry likes to sleep with his toy donkey, Eeyore. "He's good to cuddle because his head kind of goes over my arm. It's quite nice if you're feeling lonely," he confesses.
- Danny has a phobia of glass. He's always worried that he'll smash it.
- Dougie and Tom are scared of the dark.
- Harry is rubbish at chores and only washes his T-shirts once a month.
- Danny used to get told off at school for falling asleep in class all the time.
- Harry's so posh that he still calls his mum 'Mummy'. Bless!
- Tom says he'd pose naked for £100,000. Start saving those pennies!
- Harry was a naughty lad in school. He was always getting detentions for being a chatterbox in class.
- Dougie used to breed lizards.
- Danny's dad is a prison officer.
- Tom is allergic to prawns and gets really ill if he eats them.
- Dougie is brilliant at doing impressions of cartoon sound effects.
- Harry appears in Busted's video for 'Crashed The Wedding'. He runs on at the start and pushes James off the stage, and he's also in the background, drumming.
- Sometimes Dougie signs his autograph in the shape of a skateboard.
- Harry is the least hygienic of the boys. "I have to debate whether I want to have a shower or not in the morning. I won't have one if I can't be bothered."

- Danny used to strum his guitar in bed at night to help send him to sleep.
- Poor Dougie was so nervous when he auditioned for the band that he puked.
- Danny wears Calvin Klein underwear, but he's also partial to Tesco's checked pants because they're looser. "Those Kleins are pretty tight!" he says.
- Harry used to be a big scrounger at school. "I was always the one borrowing 50p to buy sweets," he confesses.
- Danny's favourite aftershave is Davidoff's Cool Water.
- Tom went to the same school as Matt from Busted – Sylvia Young's Performing Arts School. He recalls, "At lunchtime, Matt used to go out and get a massive portion of chips and then wash the whole lot down with a pint of milk!"
- The first CD Harry bought was *(What's The Story) Morning Glory* by Oasis.
- Danny's favourite part of his body is his smile. "Although when I was playing football, it was my stomach," he says.
- During the holidays, Harry used to work in a factory packing fish.
- Danny and Tom have matching star tattoos on their feet. Tom had to ask for his parents' permission before he got his done.
- The guys have some bizarre pre-gig superstitions. For example, Harry *has* to go on stage first and Dougie *has* to wear shorts.
- Tom was once an extra in *EastEnders*. He played a character called Dean.
- Danny is a self-confessed Mummy's boy. "I try to speak to her every day. She misses me playing guitar in the front room."
- Tom once appeared in a TV commercial for Curry's.
- Tom must be the only lad in the world who hates football.
- Harry loves Marmite.
- When he was eleven, Danny used to collect money for a window cleaner. "I earned about £2 every four hours. I used to run around in the freezing cold collecting his money for him," he says
- Tom hates bananas.
- Danny's favourite football team is Bolton Wanderers.
- When he was thirteen, Tom did the voice of a dog for the cartoon *Spot the Dog*.
- Dougie collects Puma trainers.
- Danny's always being mistaken for James from Busted. "It's not all bad though. I've even signed a girl's knickers because she thought I was James!"
- Harry hates his legs. "They're too skinny," he complains.
- Tom used to get into trouble at school for his wacky haircuts.
- Tom calls Harry a heifer, because he's so clumsy.
- Danny says he hates having to wear make-up. It makes his skin really itchy.

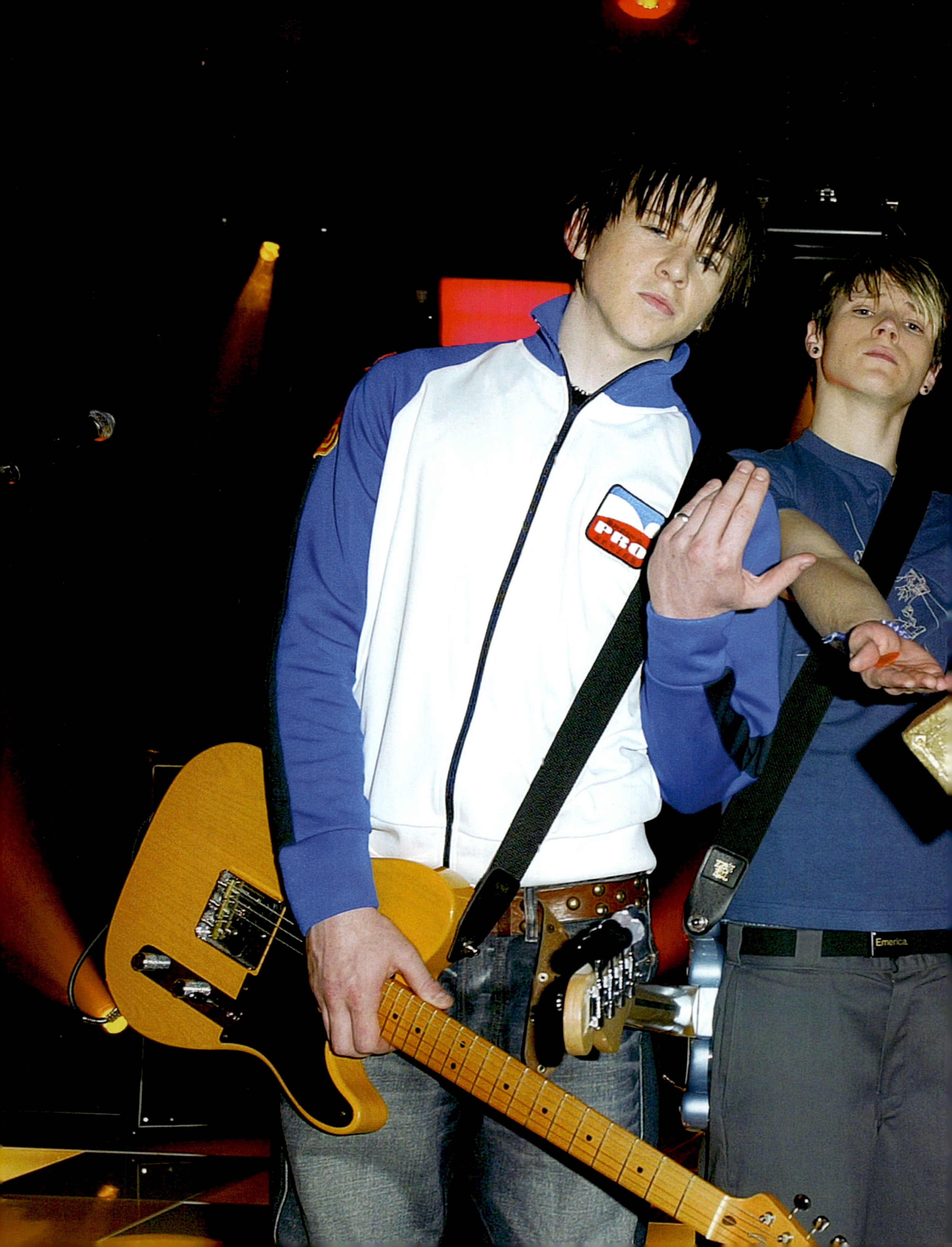
PRO
Emerica

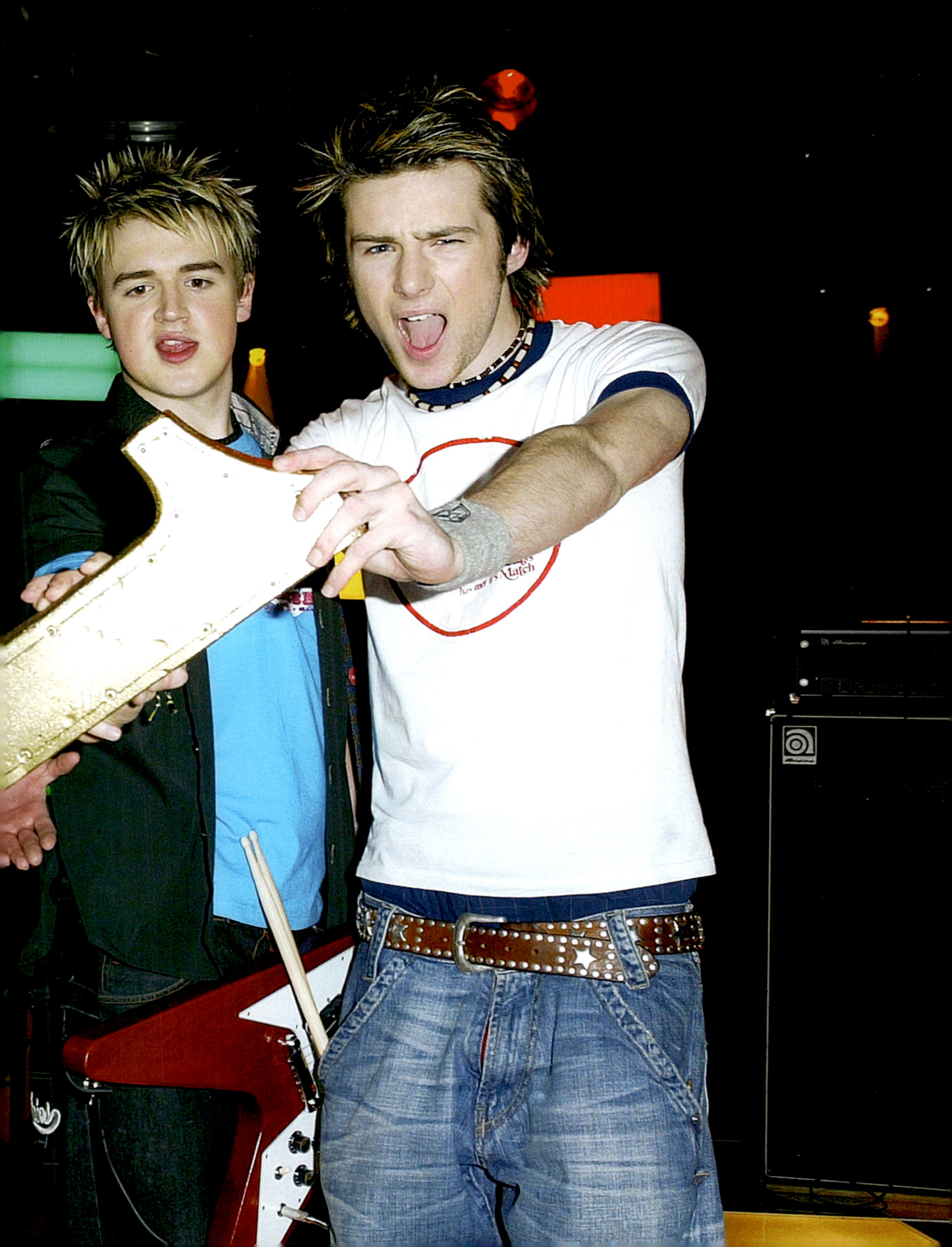

GIRLS, GIRLS, GIRLS

They may be top pin-ups, but the McFly boys still insist they find it tough to get a date. Surely that can't be true! Find out what the boys really think about girlfriends, what they look for in the ideal girl and which famous ladies they fancy...

Harry

BIGGEST TURN-ON: "I love sexy smiles and pretty eyes."
BIGGEST TURN-OFF: "Bad breath! And also if a girl is overly flirty and pushy."
FAVOURITE CHAT-UP LINE: "I don't have one, because I don't think they work!"
FAMOUS FANCIES: Surprise, surprise, Harry fancies Britney Spears. "She's so fit!" he gushes. "I think Rachel Stevens is pretty cute, too. I met her once. It was a nightmare just being in the same room as someone as gorgeous as her without screaming 'You're so fit!'. She smiled and shook my hand which was nice." He also thinks Keira Knightley is stunning.
FIRST SNOG: "A girl called Susannah when I was thirteen. But before that I was always trying to kiss matrons at prep school!"
ON SNOGGING FANS: "I have no problem with snogging fans, as long as they're not just into me because of the band."
SERIAL SNOGGER: Harry once snogged eight girls in one night! "I was having a competition with a mate," he reveals.
BIG-TIME BLUSHER: "When I was at school, my sister used to get all her friends to come round and I'd get so embarrassed. Then one person would go, 'You're going pretty red, Harry!' and I'd go even redder, and my whole body would start steaming!"
WHAT HE LOOKS FOR IN A GIRL: "Someone who's easy to talk to and doesn't have a fake laugh. And she needs to look good, too. I like a cool personality, good taste in music and clothes – I like punky or retro – and girls that make an effort."
NICEST THING HE'S DONE FOR A GIRL: "I travelled ten hours in a day just to see my girlfriend for two hours, because she was moving to Canada. The day before she left, I got up at 6 a.m. and travelled five-and-a-half hours on a train from Essex to Liverpool. I saw her for two hours and then had to come all the way back."
HE SAYS: "I'm definitely a one-girl boy."

Tom

FAMOUS FANCIES: Tom likes Nadine from Girls Aloud, but he absolutely adores the actress Katie Holmes. "I'm totally in love with her. Seriously, I have feelings for her!" He also likes Kelly Osbourne and says, "She's really cool. I'd definitely date her."

FAVOURITE CHAT-UP LINE: "I don't use chat-up lines, which might explain why I am single!"

SNOGGING SNOT ALERT: "A bogey came out of my nose when I was kissing a girl once. That's pretty embarrassing. But she didn't say anything, so I think I got away with it. I just kinda brushed it off her shoulder!"

WHAT HE LOOKS FOR IN A GIRL: "A pretty face. You decide in four seconds of meeting someone if you fancy them or not, apparently. I like girls who are casual and don't try too hard, but I hate girls with sticky lips!"

IDEAL GIRL: "She'd be fun, sexy, and fit, with a nice smile, have a cool dress sense, and excellent taste in music."

HOW TO BAG TOM: Girls, you may want to start practising your Italian, because Tom's last girlfriend was Italian, and he says that he's still good friends with her.

ROMANTIC: Tom is so obsessed with Katie Holmes, he even wrote a song about her called 'Ladder By My Window'. And does it involve Miss Holmes creeping into his bedroom after dark by any chance? Duh! Of course it does! "Well yes, it is about a fantasy!" he admits.

PERSONALITY OR LOOKS?: "I honestly prefer a good personality. I went out with a girl once who was gorgeous, but she had a really lame attitude. After a couple of weeks I just couldn't take it any more."

NICEST THING HE'S DONE FOR A GIRL: "I pretended to cook lasagne for a girl, but really I got my mum to cook it!"

HE SAYS: "I usually get stuck with the girl that no one else fancies. I'm the loner of the band. That'd be my lonely hearts advert – 'If you like a guy with no mates and no dress sense, I'm your man'!"

Dougie

BIGGEST TURN-ON: "Girls in thongs!"

FAVOURITE CHAT-UP LINE: "I ain't got a favourite chat-up line. That's why I haven't got a girlfriend!"

SNOGTASTIC: He once kissed four girls at a friend's birthday party.

FAMOUS FANCIES: He has a crush on Frankie from S Club 8. "I just wish she'd ask me out on a date, because she's so fit. She's only about a year younger than me, too! Oh, and Hilary Duff rocks! I totally love American girls."

SHY BOY: "I freak out every time I'm with a girl that I think is fit. I'm such a loser when it comes to girls, I'm really shy and quiet."

ON DATING: "I'd love to date. I wish I could just get at least one date! If I had a girlfriend I liked, I'd hang on to her."
WHAT HE LOOKS FOR IN A GIRL: "I'm not bothered when it comes to hair colour or stuff like that. I just like a girl who's easy-going and open-minded musically."
PERSONALITY OR LOOKS?: "Call me greedy, but I go for both!"
HE SAYS: "Girls are the most important things on the planet. Men may bring in the money, but women give birth."

Danny

SERIAL SNOGGER: He once kissed nineteen girls in the same night as part of a bet!
ON BEING FAITHFUL: "I'd snog different girls if I was seeing someone casually, but not if we were going out properly."
WHY HE'D MAKE A GOOD BOYFRIEND: "I'd treat my girlfriend nice. I can never argue, and I can never start an argument either."
GIRL HATES: The only thing he hates about girls is when they make fun of him. "I find it so heart-wrenching when you meet a girl and you know she's perfect for you but she's like, 'I don't want to go out with you'."
FAMOUS FANCIES: Danny has a huge crush on Heidi from the Sugababes.
PERFECT DATE: "Maybe an amazing concert. If I want to be romantic, I dim the lights and put on some music, but I'm not cheesy. I have given a girl a teddy bear with 'I love you' on it before – but I was in primary school!"
WHAT HE LOOKS FOR IN A GIRL: "It'd be brilliant if she knew about music so I could play her my songs and she could give me her opinion."
GIRL HISTORY: "I've only been out with five girls, and they were all quite serious relationships. The longest lasted about two months!"
COWARD: He once dumped a girl by avoiding her phone calls. According to Danny – "She was doing my head in!"
NICEST THING HE'S DONE FOR A GIRL: "I used to run six miles to this girl's house every morning before college, just so I could see her for a couple of hours."
PERSONALITY OR LOOKS?: "Well, I have to look at her, so it has to be looks!"
HE SAYS: "I can't get a girlfriend at all. I'll chat up anybody, and I'd definitely snog a fan!"

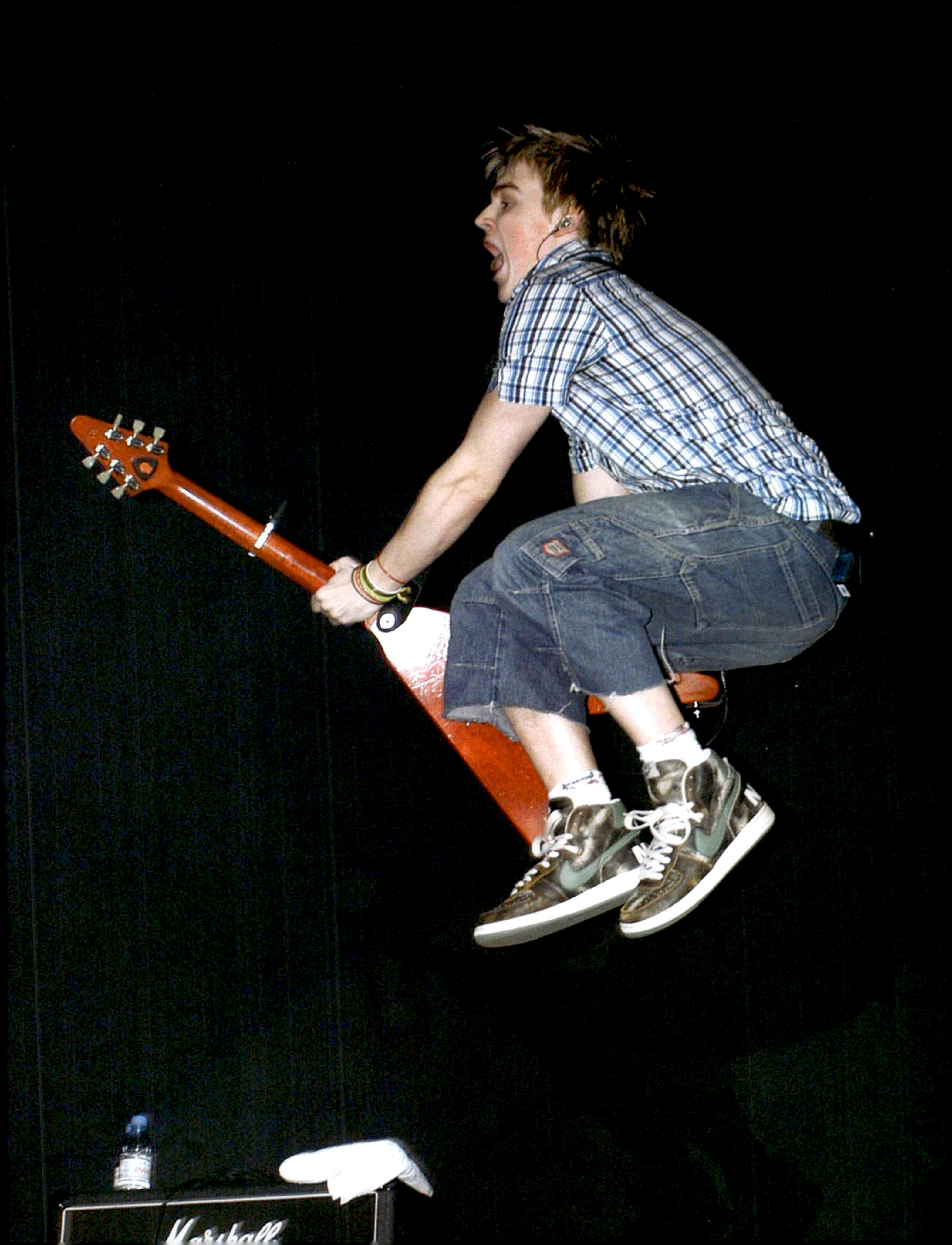
Marshall

WHO'S FOR YOU?

Answer these questions and find out which of the McFly boys is for you.

1. On your first date you go to the cinema, but what kind of film do you choose?
A. A real mind-puzzler with lots of surprising twists and turns.
B. A laugh-out-loud comedy with lots of funny lines that you can use afterwards.
C. A good old-fashioned, heart-warming film with a happy ending.
D. A movie packed with toilet humour!

2. How would you describe your boyfriend's bedroom?
A. It's tidy and spacious, but there are far too many posters of Katie Holmes on the walls!
B. Minging! There are empty pizza boxes lying next to piles of smelly socks. But there are some cute cuddly toys on the bed.
C. Packed with guitar equipment and a huge record collection of old rock-and-roll.
D. Quite girlie for a boy's room, with flowery curtains like you'd find at your gran's house.

3. You meet your boyfriend's mate for the first time. What does he say?
A. "Want to check out my extensive collection of Beach Boys' memorabilia?"
B. "Jolly good to meet you! One has heard so many wonderful things about you."
C. "Hi, my name's James. I'm in a band called Busted, but everyone thinks that your boyfriend and I are the same person!"
D. "Dude! Like, it's totally rad to finally get to meet you. High five!"

4. It's your boyfriend's birthday. What do you buy him to wear?
A. Anything that involves at least five colours.
B. A baggy hooded jumper by a really cool skater label.
C. A vintage T-shirt with a picture of his favourite band on it.
D. A pair of really oversized shorts, that hang so low you can see his boxers!

5. You ask your boy to express how much he loves you. What does he do?
A. Writes you a really romantic love song and sings it to you on a clear night under the moon and stars.
B. Tells you that you're a million times prettier than any girl he's ever gone out with, and that you've got a really fit body.
C. Arranges a candlelit dinner for just the two of you, and gives you a promise ring with his name engraved inside it.

D. Puts on his best American cartoon voice and shouts, Girlfriend, you rock my world!

6. You think your McFly fella is the picture of perfection. What does he think of himself?
A. "I'm the least sexiest person in the world."
B. "My legs are too skinny."
C. "I wish my stomach was more toned."
D. "I hate my knobbly knees."

7. You're thinking about getting a new hairstyle. What does your guy say?
A. "Get five colours in your hair."
B. "I don't mind really, just so long as it doesn't hide that sexy face of yours!"
C. "Grow it. I love girls with long hair, kinda like Heidi from Sugababes."
D. "Bleach it platinum blonde and have it really spiky. Then we'll match!"

WHO'S YOUR McFLY MAN?

Now, count up how many As, Bs, Cs and Ds you got and find out below what this means.

Mostly As – Tom
You and Tom are a match made in heaven! He's the ideal guy to take home to your parents. He really knows how to make a girl feel good about herself and believe that she's the most important person in the world. If you like being treated like a queen, you'll love being with Tom. You just can't lose!

Mostly Bs – Harry
You like your totty to be a bit classy! OK, VERY classy! His impeccable manners are simply the sexiest thing in the world and those big blue eyes make you melt. You and Harry will love having a laugh and watching a film with Jim Carrey in it. Don't worry if he's feeling a bit slobbish – you love him for his imperfections as well as his many perfections!

Mostly Cs – Danny
Change your name to Mrs Jones, because you and Danny are simply meant to be together. You love Northern lads like Danny – a bit rough and tough, but at the same time a fella who isn't afraid to show his softer side. With romantic gestures like candlelit dinners and watching soppy films with you, he'll be your boyfriend and best friend all in one!

Mostly Ds – Dougie
You and Dougie are the ultimate Dude and Dudette! You share the same cheeky sense of humour, and you are both totally obsessed with American culture. Let's face it, your ideal date would probably consist of crowd surfing at a Blink 182 gig! You love lads who are innocent looking, with cute features and who aren't afraid of acting the fool – just to see you smile.

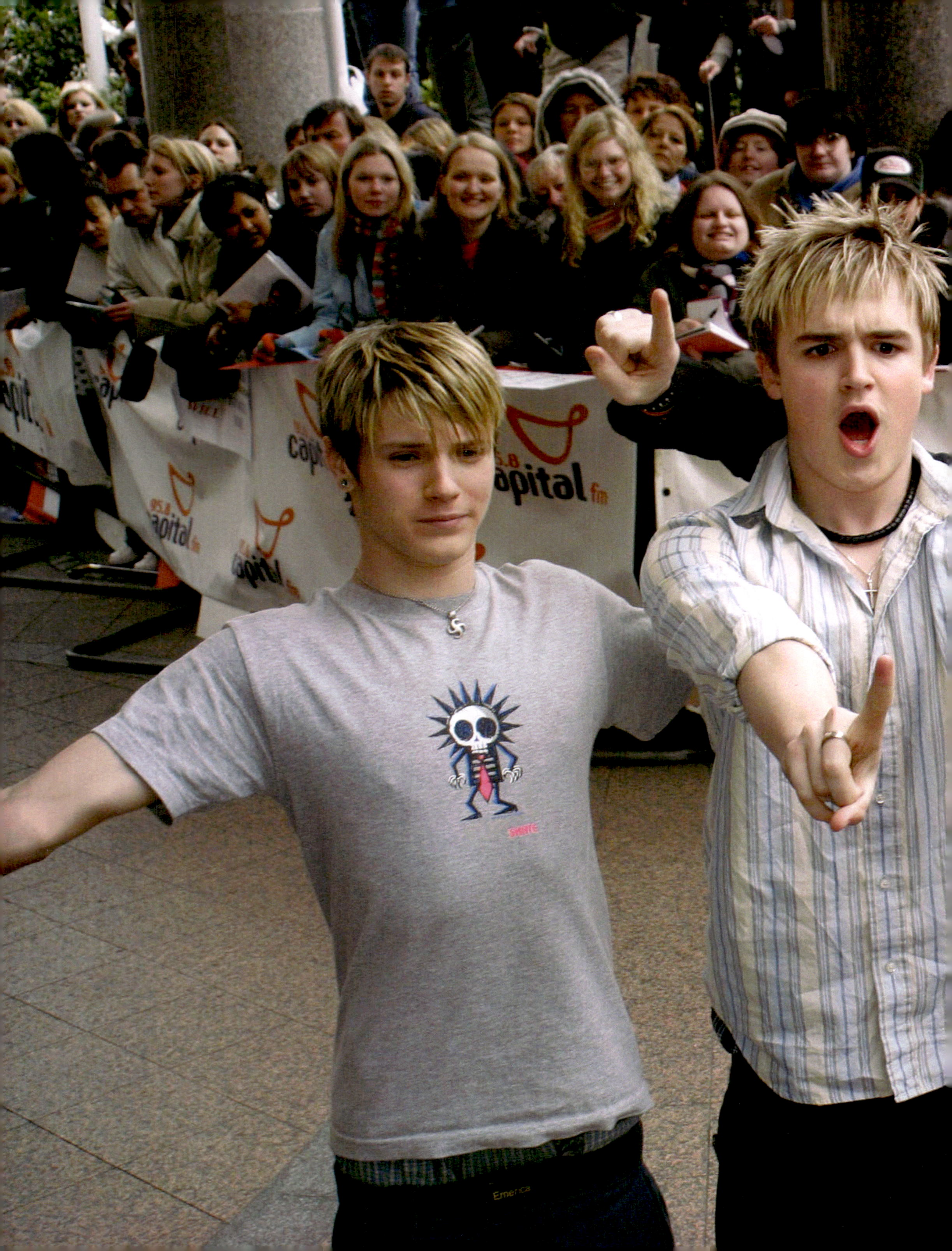
capital fm
Emerica

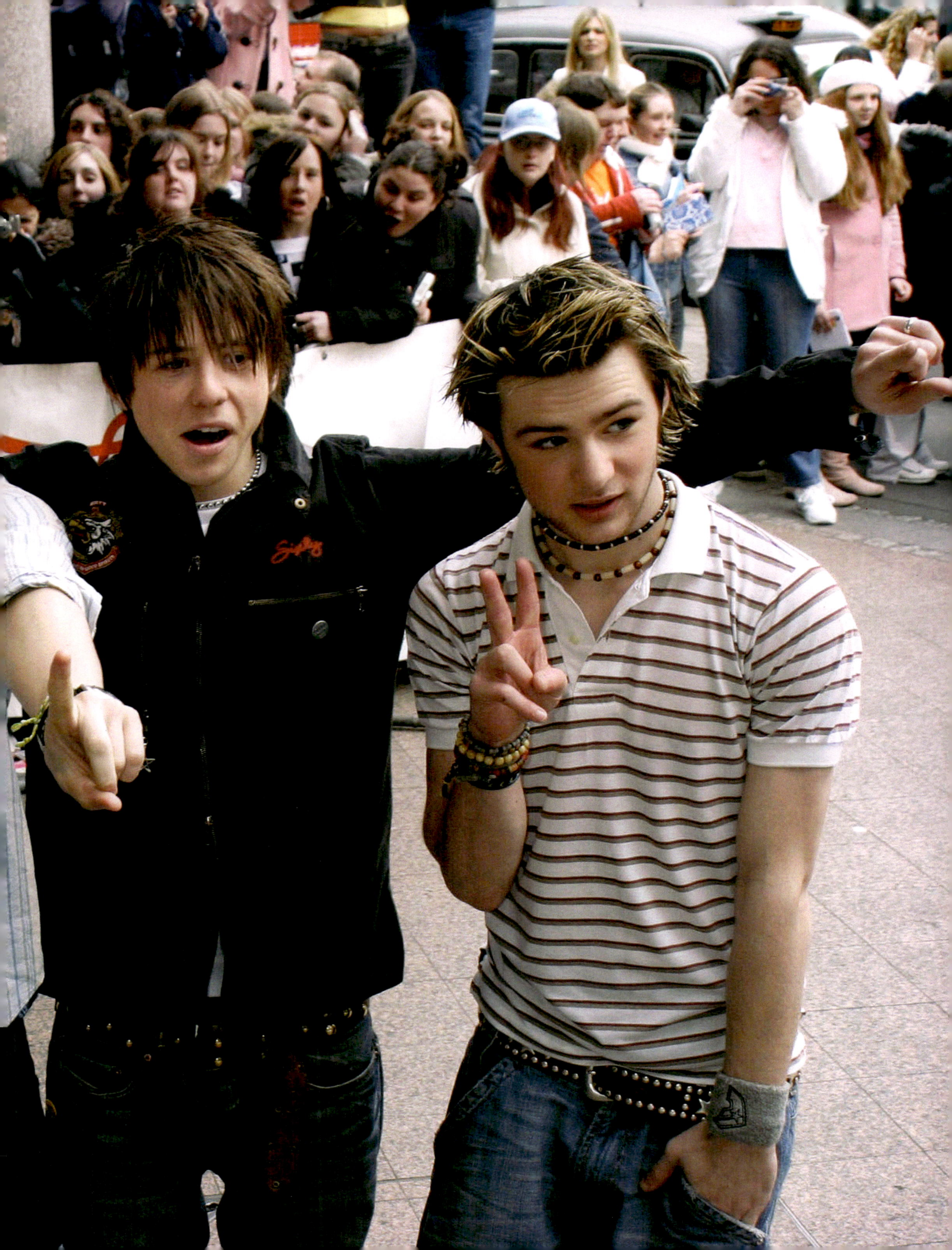

STYLE SECRETS

With their baggy shorts, oversized T-shirts and clumpy skater shoes, McFly have the edgy punk look down to perfection. This section reveals all you need to know about the McFly boys' style.

Tom

Tom reckons he hasn't got a single ounce of fashion sense in him and that he's easily the least fashionable member of the band. "I've always been someone who doesn't really care what they wear," he admits.

He favours loud colours, wacky styles and has a far more eccentric taste in clothes than the other lads. He likes collecting one-off T-shirts with weird and wonderful logos on them. One of his favourites is his Incredible Hulk T-shirt that he got in Florida. "It's even got muscles that stick out on it. It's cool!"

It sounds like there's no such thing as a boring clothes day when you're Tom. However, the other lads are never in too much of a hurry to borrow anything from his wardrobe, as Tom will tell you. "I've got these really loud multi-coloured beach shorts," he says. "I like to wear them with a bright green T-shirt. The other boys think they're horrible!"

Tom reckons he's a minus ten when it comes to his looks. "I think I'm the least sexy person on the planet, but I'm ten out of ten for cool!" Nothing like a bit of modesty! And he wishes that he looked like Hollywood hunk Chris Klein, but only because he's Katie Holmes' boyfriend!

Danny

Danny hates shopping, so it's just as well that the band has stylists on hand to help out the boys whenever they need it. "In the mornings I always think, should I wear something different, because I wear the same clothes every day? Or should I just ring the stylists and nick some clothes from them? It's just so much easier than having to go shopping!" he raves.

Danny loves wearing retro clothes, especially cool 50s-style bomber jackets. He also likes big, cosy, hooded jumpers.

He wears cool, chunky belt buckles that are customized and say words like 'rock' or 'McFly' on them.

There is a smarter side to Danny. He says his style icon is David Beckham, and before he was in McFly he used to don a sharper look. "I did have the whole Charlie-Busted-blazer-look going on," he reveals. "But I've ditched it now. I mostly wear jeans, retro T-shirts and other weird shirts!"

Danny doesn't mind discussing style, but he doesn't like to dwell on his looks. "I'm the second most unsexy person in this band. I'm a one out of ten! I don't think we're good looking, I think we're just cool," he says. But even this cool fella has had his fair share of fashion mistakes! "I once wore these really tight black trousers with a bright red shirt. The shirt was so long, it came down past my knees!'

Harry

Harry is the posh boy in the band, but that doesn't mean he wears designer labels. His style is boho-chic. He enjoys wearing baggy jeans or cords, old school sneakers, and wristbands, of which he has loads. He loves beaded necklaces and bracelets.

Harry doesn't rate himself very highly at all. "Seriously, we are the least sexy people in the world! We're not sexy, trust me!"

Harry is just effortlessly cool. "What you see us wearing is what we would wear anyway. It's what we're comfortable in." The only hang-up he has is having to wear make-up! "I look at myself and think, 'Jeez, I'm a woman!', but I suppose make-up makes you look better."

Dougie

According to Dougie, no one really liked him at school, because he dressed differently from everyone else. Dougie's style is the ultimate skater dude. He definitely wouldn't look out of place at a rock festival in California. He practically lives in long shorts or skater pants, and rarely wears trousers.

Dougie's feet are often kitted out in chunky skater trainers by DC Shoes, and he has an extensive collection of cool T-shirts by brands such as Dickies, Vans and Billabong, as well as band T-shirts such as Blink 182 and New Found Glory. But his favourite T-shirts are the ones with the Attica logo – the logo of the company owned by his punk heroes Blink 182.

"I don't think we dress in a really sexy way... we're hot, sweaty guitarists!" laughs Dougie.

CRINGE! MCFLY

Cover your eyes if you scare easily. Here are some of McFly's most cringe-worthy confessions!

Tom

• "I went to a celeb bash with James from Busted, but we couldn't get home, so we sneaked into a hotel and slept in the corridor. But the manager caught us and booted us out!"

• "I ran into a newsagents looking for a magazine with Katie Holmes in it, but they didn't have it and, as I ran out, I crashed straight into one of those signs they have, that stand on the floor and flap in the wind. The shopkeeper came out and told me off for ruining his sign, but the worst thing was, it was right outside a pub and everyone saw me!"

Dougie

- "I think my most embarrassing moment has to be when I blocked up our toilet with a monster poo, which we later named Jeff!"
- "I'm not as innocent as everyone thinks I am. I used to be in this pop punk band called Ataiz, and I once played a gig wearing just my boxer shorts!"
- "I accidentally swear all the time on live TV. This one time, I hit my guitar against a wall and just went 'bleep!'."

Danny

- "This one time, I was in an exam and it was dead quiet, and then I sneezed and farted all at the same time. It was so loud!"
- "Me and my mate met two fit girls from Scotland on holiday once, and we arranged to meet them later. After we finished talking I walked off backwards, tripped up and fell over the kerb on to my bum!"
- "I used to go boxing every week, and after a year or so my trainer put me in for my first ever fight. It was a big event, and loads of my family and friends came to watch me. But then I saw the guy I was supposed to be fighting. He was only fifteen, but he must have been about seven foot tall! I'm afraid to say I was wimpy and bottled out!"

Harry

- "I'm always falling up the stairs at home. Tom calls me 'heifer', because I always knock things over when I sit down on the sofa. I'm just a bit clumsy, that's all!"
- "Once I pricked a girl with a thorn in the playground and she started crying. I said someone else had done it, but she came up to me and shouted, 'It was you!' – I was busted!"

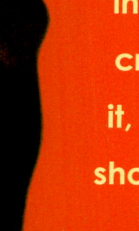

ORIGINAL PRANKSTERS

They may look like butter wouldn't melt in their mouths, but behind those angelic smiles lurk some very wild boys! Check out their crazy stunts and hilarious pranks.

Cheeky moments

Harry confesses that he once stripped in front of his mates and ran around his hotel room naked on a school holiday!

Danny is a serial mooner and used to flash his bum at passing strangers as he went by on his football team bus.

Dougie got into trouble with his teachers for sticking a batch of stickers all over the school. "The teachers weren't happy," he confesses. We bet they weren't!

Danny used to make prank phone calls, pretending to sell magazines. "People always fell for it because I was so good at accents," he boasts.

Harry once got drunk at school. "The last time I puked was probably at Uppingham, when I was drunk on a Saturday night."

Tom

"We had a week of watching horror films and we watched *The Ring*, which is really frightening. When the phone rings in the film, you know someone's going to get killed, so as soon as the film finished and while it was still pitch black, I got my mobile out and dialled the house number. Everyone was so scared!"

Dougie

"Danny gets me into trouble. He's into going to clubs and he never tells me there is an age limit. So I get to the door and the bouncer tells me I can't go in! He's been trying to teach me how to look older."

"I once dressed up in girl's clothes – it was so funny!"

Harry

"I was a cheeky brat at school, but the teachers liked me. Once I sneaked out of class to play basketball, and I ran into a window that someone was opening. I had to have twenty-five stitches! I didn't get any sympathy because I was meant to be in class."

"Once my brother, my mates and I dived off a roof into a pond in the middle of winter. I also once jumped into some manure, which wasn't very pleasant at all! I wouldn't recommend it!"

Danny

"We had this teacher at our school called Mr Graham. Everyone was throwing tennis balls behind his back that just missed, then I got this massive football and threw it at him – and it hit his head! I got three detentions. It didn't help that I was laughing when I got told off!"

"We tend to muck around quite a lot. This one time Tom fell asleep in the studio, so we put the mic right up his nose and recorded his snoring. It was so loud! We were going to draw on his face, but we thought he might get a bit cross!"

"I got in trouble with the police by accident once. Me and my cousin were taking a short cut through a factory, but the place was being burgled at the time and, unknown to us, was surrounded by police. When we came out the other side, they nicked us, thinking we were the burglars. It was well scary."

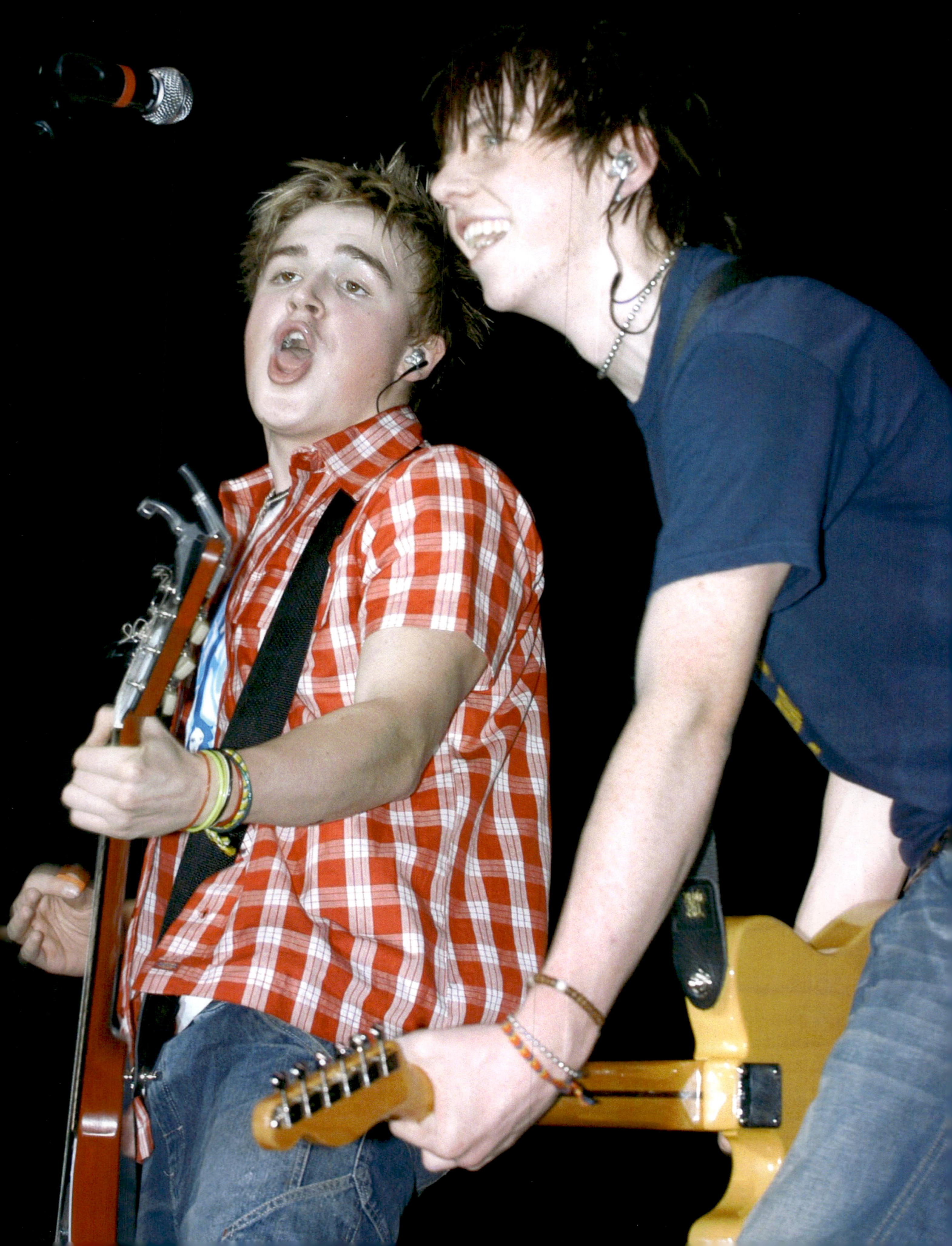

McFAN OR McPHONEY

Test your McFly knowledge with this quick quiz! Then check your answers on page 61.

1. What's the name of the posh boarding school Harry used to attend?

2. Which animal did Dougie use to breed?

3. What's Danny's favourite film?

4. Which member of McFly has a crush on Frankie from S Club 8?

5. What's the name of Tom's favourite band?

6. Complete the lyrics from '5 Colours In Her Hair':
"The rumour's spreading round that she ____ in the ____!"

7. Which member of McFly sleeps with a stuffed toy donkey?

8. What's Dougie's favourite word?

9. Which band did Tom miss out on a place in?

10. How long did '5 Colours In Her Hair' stay at number one?

11. What's Harry's favourite drink?

12. Where was Dougie born?

13. Who spent £4,000 on a studio with his first pay cheque?

14. Which member of McFly was the first to pass his driving test?

15. Tom went to school with which member of Busted?

16. Danny and Tom have matching star tattoos, but where are they?

17. Which member of McFly likes to eat dead skin?

18. Who's Dougie's favourite female singer?

19. What's the name of the character that Tom played in *EastEnders*?

20. Which member of McFly supports Bolton Wanderers football team?

59

BACK TO THE FUTURE

McFly were named after a character from the 1980s cult movie *Back To The Future*, but what does the future hold for the four boys? We took a mystical look at Tom, Harry, Dougie and Danny's star signs to see what the next twelve months hold for them...

Tom
STAR SIGN: Cancer
GOOD TRAITS: Reliable, intelligent, in control
BAD TRAITS: A worrier, over-critical, fussy
PREDICTIONS: Tom will lead the band on to achieving the best they can. A positive year lies ahead for him, but he must be careful not to become over-confident and let the success go to his head. He will control his bossy mood swings and learn to worry less, too. He'll take on extra responsibility with outside projects and continue songwriting for other bands. He may think about buying his own property and he'll treat himself to that dream car he's always wanted! However, he won't need a flashy motor to impress the girls. This charming young man will find it tough to find the girl he's been searching for, someone who's faithful and genuine. But that doesn't mean he won't experience a little romance along the way. He definitely won't be short of offers!

Danny
STAR SIGN: Pisces
GOOD TRAITS: Good with money, kind and lively
BAD TRAITS: A perfectionist, possessive, jealous
PREDICTIONS: Danny's year will be packed with lots of partying! But he must be careful he doesn't burn out or turn into one of those celebs who turns up to the opening of an envelope! He's going to enjoy the fruits of his labour and treat himself to even more studio equipment and build himself a mini-empire! He'll work hard at making sure McFly remain at the top of the charts and he'll enjoy experimenting with new sounds for their next album. He'll throw himself into songwriting, but he'll be in his element as the lads embark on their very own headlining tour. He'll experience new things, visit new countries and get a taste of the life of a rock-and-roll band!

Harry

STAR SIGN: Capricorn
GOOD TRAITS: Down-to-earth, efficient, hard-working
BAD TRAITS: Slow, stubborn, dominant
PREDICTIONS: Harry will flirt his way through the next year as he meets lots of gorgeous girls, especially celebrity types! He'll swap numbers on many occasions and be happy casually dating a string of beauties. However, he'll stumble across a few personal problems. He'll be shocked to discover he can no longer indulge in certain things that he used to before the band. He'll realize that he's no longer just a regular teenage boy. He may become slightly upset with the lack of privacy and betrayal of old school chums, but he won't need to look far for someone to cheer him up, because his band mates will be there through thick and thin!

Dougie

STAR SIGN: Sagittarius
GOOD TRAITS: Modest, honest, humble
BAD TRAITS: Cautious, inconsistent, insecure
PREDICTIONS: Over the following twelve months, Dougie will gradually come out of his shell and reach a degree of comfort with his new-found fame with McFly. He'll learn to relax around strangers and open up a bit more, but he'll still remain wary of people he doesn't fully know, and he'll still find it difficult to trust people. He'll receive a lot more female attention and, as daunting as that may seem to him at the moment, he'll come to terms with this. His painfully shy ways will give way to a growth of confidence with the ladies. Dougie's role in the band will increase, as he tries his hand at songwriting and even surprises himself with what he's capable of achieving.

Whatever happens in the coming months, on thing is absolutely certain for the McFly boys – that we'll be with them every step of the way!

Answers to the crossword on page 35

ACROSS
1. Sagittarius
2. MTV
3. Pizza
4. Dimple
7. Kerry
9. Homodom
10. Cat
13. Ukulele
14. Bongo drums

DOWN
1. Skateboard
5. Puked
6. Art
8. Colours
10. Cleaner
11. Heidi
12. March

Answers to the quick quiz on page 59

1. Uppingham
2. Lizards
3. E.T.
4. Dougie
5. The Beach Boys
6. "The rumour's spreading round that she COOKS in the NUDE!"
7. Harry
8. Rad
9. Busted
10. weeks
11. Apple juice
12. Orsett
13. Danny
14. Tom
15. Matt
16. On their feet
17. Dougie
18. Amy Lee from Evanescence
19. Dean
20. Danny

61